Contents

A great showman . . . .

Who was Houdini? 6

Getting into magic 10

Moving to escapology. 14

Managing danger. 22

Trickery 25

Inventions and ideas 33

Is that all? 36

How did Houdini die? 41

After Houdini 42

Glossary. 46

Index 47

A great showman

Have you heard of Harry Houdini? He was the world's most famous escapologist. He was so good at escaping, and so fast, that some people thought he had magic powers.

Houdini did lots of really dangerous things. Do NOT copy him! Anyone without his training and skill could be seriously hurt.

What's an escapologist?

It's a performer who specialises in escaping from things.

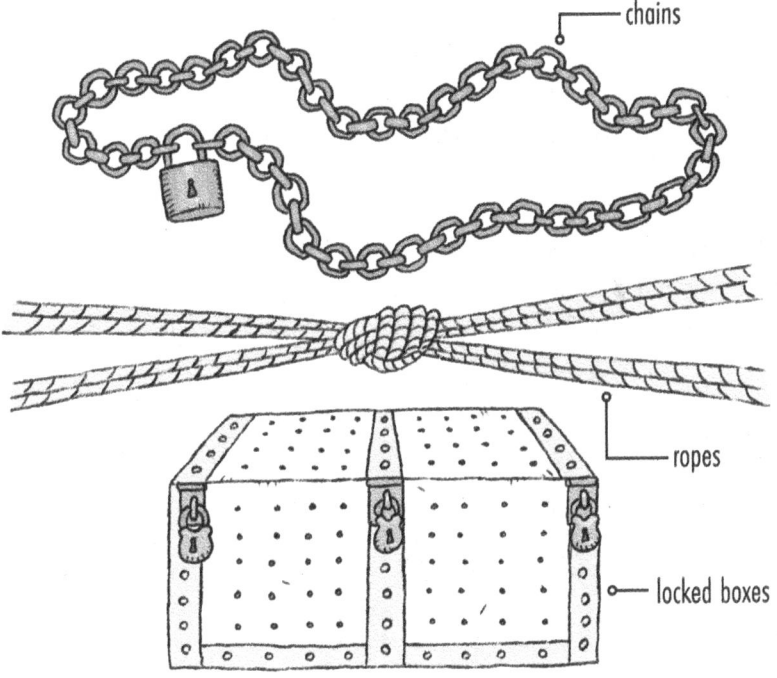

Houdini was a brilliant showman. He invented new ways of dazzling his audience, and practised and trained to perform his **stunts** perfectly. But he was many things besides a performer.

Houdini was a famous American, who was born in Hungary. He invented stunts and the machinery for them, and lots more besides. He even invented his own name! He lived an extraordinary life, and has become so legendary that some of the things people think they know about him aren't even true!

But escapology acts aren't based entirely on truth. They rely on trickery, at least partly. They give the audience the thrill of danger, while reassuring them that the performer should be all right in the end. So watch out for half-truths and trickery! Here is the story of Houdini.

Who was Houdini?

Houdini started life as Erik Weisz. He was born in Budapest, Hungary, on 24th March 1874. His father was a **rabbi** and Erik was one of eight children, with six brothers and a sister.

Erik's family moved to the USA when he was four, and he grew up in the state of Wisconsin. The family changed how their names were spelled, to look more American. So Erik Weisz became Ehrich Weiss, but his famous name was still a long way off.

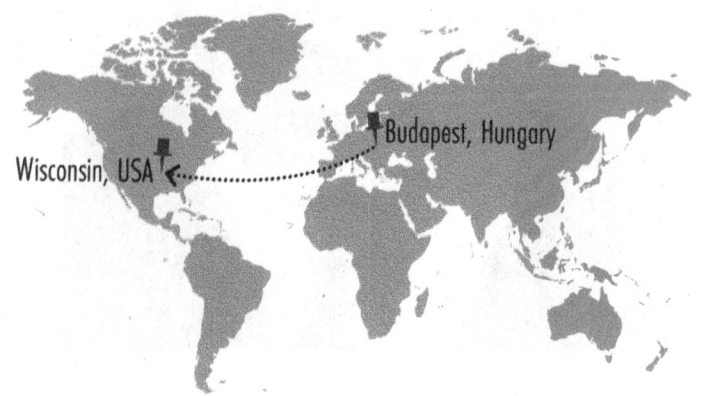

Ehrich's father lost his job in 1882, which left the family short of money. This may have been why Ehrich started performing at a circus.

At the age of nine, he appeared as a trapeze artist. He called himself 'The Prince of the Air', showing how confident he was in his abilities. People said that he was so flexible, he could bend over backwards and pick things up off the floor with his teeth!

In 1887, Ehrich's family moved to New York. Ehrich was based there for the rest of his life, even though he travelled a lot of the time.

Ehrich found a part-time job to help his family until his father could find more work. In fact, he had up to four jobs at once. The story of how he got one of these jobs shows us his confidence again.

There was a queue of people waiting to ask about a job cutting out ties. Fifteen-year-old Ehrich walked up and down, telling everyone that the post had already been taken. When all the others had gone, Ehrich walked into the factory. He was the only one left, so of course he got the job!

On top of his jobs, Ehrich took up sports at weekends. He trained at local athletics clubs, and did well in running, boxing and swimming. He became very fit and carried on exercising all his life.

Ehrich was a successful competitor, as this story from 1890 shows. A teenage runner saw that Ehrich was listed to run in a race near New York. This boy rushed home, saying that Ehrich Weiss was taking part, so there was no point in running!

Ehrich used to show off his running medals, though some of them looked like he might have made them himself.

Getting into magic

When he was 16, Ehrich read a newspaper article about the French magician Jean Robert-Houdin. He was so interested, he bought Robert-Houdin's **autobiography**, and read it over and over.

Robert-Houdin had changed the way magic tricks were performed. Before him, performances were very slow and serious.

Robert-Houdin decided that it was more interesting for his audience if he moved around more. He even invited people to join him on stage. Possibly his most famous trick was when he appeared to send his son to sleep and then made him 'float in the air' in front of the audience.

Ehrich was already spending a lot of time working on coin and card tricks. He started performing as 'Eric the Great'. Then, in 1891, he moved on to performing with a friend from the tie factory.

This friend, Jake, said that adding -i to the end of Houdin would mean 'like Houdin'. This would be a way of showing respect for the Frenchman who had inspired them. So they performed as 'The Brothers Houdini'.

At the same time, Ehrich changed his family nickname Ehrie to the more American name Harry. That was the start of his life as Harry Houdini.

When Harry was 18, his father died. The family was really short of money so Harry had to find better-paid work.

He teamed up with his brother Theo at a big carnival in Chicago. They watched other performers there, worked on making their act exciting, and learned how to attract people to come and watch them.

Their best trick was called Metamorphosis.

Harry stood in a sack inside a trunk. Theo tied the sack shut.

Audience members helped him lock the trunk and tie ropes around it.

Then Theo pulled up a curtain, hiding himself and the trunk.

When the curtain fell, Harry was standing there.

Unlocking the trunk revealed Theo in the sack!

How did it work? Look at pages 31 to 32!

In 1894, Houdini married Wilhemina Beatrice Rahner, known as Bess. Houdini wasn't very tall, but Bess was even shorter. So when she became his assistant, the Metamorphosis effect was even more surprising, as a man changed places with a much smaller woman. They performed together in a travelling circus and Metamorphosis was always their final trick, which the whole act built up to.

Moving to escapology

Metamorphosis was the first trick in Harry's move to performing escapes and becoming famous around the world. As an escapologist, he learned how to undo handcuffs without using a key, and to escape from **straitjackets**.

Harry practised hard, because escaping from some **restraints** needed the skills of a magician. Other escapes required strength and flexibility, so he also made sure he stayed very fit.

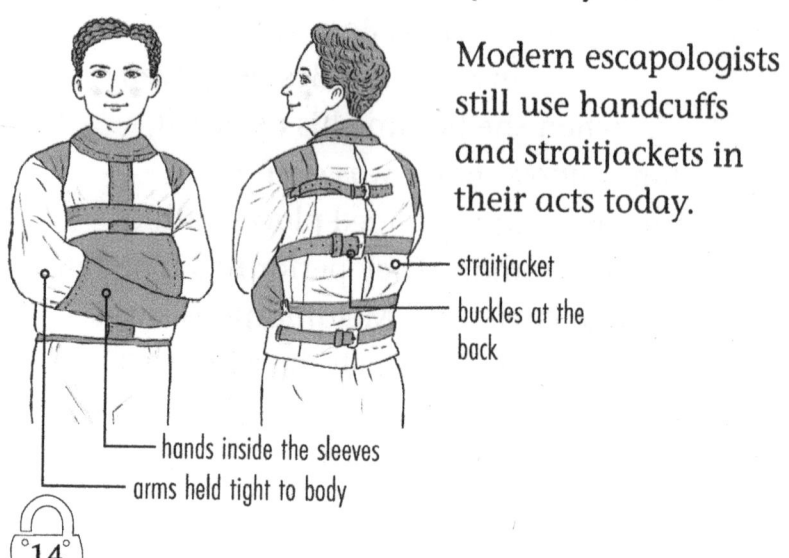

Modern escapologists still use handcuffs and straitjackets in their acts today.

- straitjacket
- buckles at the back
- hands inside the sleeves
- arms held tight to body

When they first started performing, Houdini and Bess struggled to make a living. But in 1899, their fortunes changed. Harry's escapology act was booked on a tour of theatres in the USA and Canada, and he and Bess could stop worrying about money.

An important part of the new act was that Harry challenged anyone to lock him up, and then escaped. Whatever handcuffs or padlocks they brought along, he could get out of them.

By 1900, Harry and Bess were off to Britain, and they toured in Europe for five years.

When he arrived in a new city, Houdini went to the local police headquarters and offered to break out of a **cell**. Of course he invited journalists, because he wanted lots of publicity.

A newspaper reported this stunt in Chicago on 5 April 1900. The head police officer agreed to handcuff and chain Houdini and lock him in a cell, but he reckoned that Houdini must be going to sneak in some keys. He insisted that Houdini must perform the trick without clothes, so that he couldn't smuggle anything in! Despite this, it took Houdini only about three minutes to escape.

Do NOT mess about with keys and locks!

Houdini's stunts required a lot of equipment, so he always had to travel with huge amounts of luggage. He once said that he never left home without about 40 separate items.

Houdini invited local people to challenge him in his shows. Carpenters would nail him into crates, and a blacksmith even invented his own handcuffs for a challenge. Houdini escaped from them all, getting publicity for everyone involved.

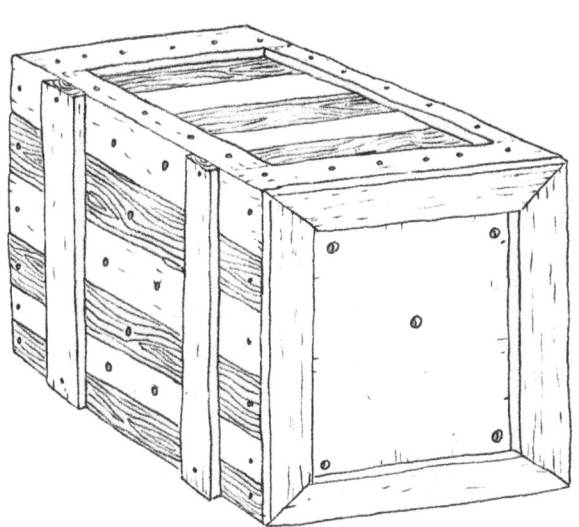

Houdini did lots of stunts that were dangerous even for someone as strong and well trained as he was. He also realised that more people came to watch him if they thought he was risking his life, so he made sure his stunts looked as dangerous as possible.

His straitjacket escapes were a way for Houdini to show off his skills, so he did them in full view of the audience. He wriggled around the stage, easing his arms over his head until he could free them enough to undo the buckles behind him. The audiences were impressed by his strength and flexibility.

To make the straitjacket escapes look more dangerous, Houdini started performing them in mid-air, suspended from a building crane. Too much never seemed to be enough, when it came to thrilling his audience.

Of course he was injured from time to time, as you would expect. But he did show some sense: when another performer died doing a dangerous trick that Houdini wanted to perform, Houdini changed his mind and dropped the trick from his act.

Thank goodness for that!

Houdini also worked on his conjuring tricks. One of his most spectacular tricks involved making an elephant 'vanish' from a tent on stage.

Houdini became more famous as he toured and took on more challenges. He got himself packaged in crates and other things, which he escaped from without damaging them. The bigger the challenge seemed to be, the louder the audience cheered.

This all led to Houdini's most impressive escapology act, which he called the Upside Down. It involved a specially made tank of water, which he was lowered into with his hands chained and his feet trapped into the lid. Then the top was bolted on.

Once Houdini was locked in the tank, a curtain was drawn and the crowd waited ... and waited ... and waited. Two minutes ticked by, then three ... and at last he appeared from behind the curtain. The crowd went wild with applause and cheering.

The escape actually took less than a minute, but Houdini wanted a big reaction. He let time pass, to build the audience's fear ... and their relief at his escape. The Upside Down became his most famous trick.

Managing danger

Houdini made the most of the danger he was in when performing his escapes. But how did he make sure he was actually safe?

First of all, he trained very hard, to make sure he was fitter than almost anyone around. Like any magician, he also practised all the skills he needed, again and again.

> ⚠️ *In this trick, Houdini is tied up and hanging high in the air – which makes it even more dangerous! Definitely NOT one to try at home.*

Another thing Houdini practised was using tiny tools to open all kinds of locks, and he could even do this with his toes.

For some tricks, he kept a tool hidden in his curly hair. Sometimes when he was about to perform an escape, he would shake hands with everyone, and kiss his wife. That was a perfect opportunity for someone to pass him a tool at the last minute.

Because he practised so hard, he could wriggle his way out of all sorts of tricky places.

In fact, Houdini's strength was important in another way.

He often invited members of the audience to help tie him up or put chains on him. Just before they began, he would swell his chest and tense all his muscles. But why would he do that?

It made him a little bit bigger all over. When he breathed out and relaxed his muscles, the ties became looser, giving him room to start wriggling out.

This was part of the final ingredient, which he pretended he never used … trickery.

Trickery

All magic relies on elements of trickery, and escapology is no different. A performer's skill makes the audience believe they're seeing something that cannot be true.

One way Houdini did this was by emphasising the parts of his act that were real. Houdini's brother Theo was still performing too, and he realised how important this was.

When Theo did a straitjacket escape behind a curtain, the audience didn't seem impressed. They thought he was tricking them, even though he wasn't.

So both brothers took to performing these escapes in full view. It helped them pretend that there was no trickery anywhere in their shows.

Here's a trick you can learn yourself, to see how magicians' trickery works. You're going to do the French Drop and make a coin disappear!

this way up, with coin above palm of hand

Take the coin between the thumb and index finger of one hand.

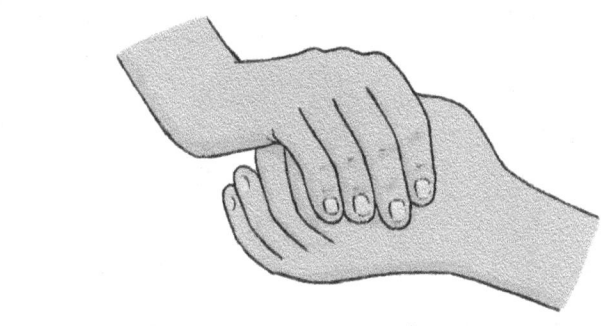

Now bring your other hand down and put your fingers over the coin.

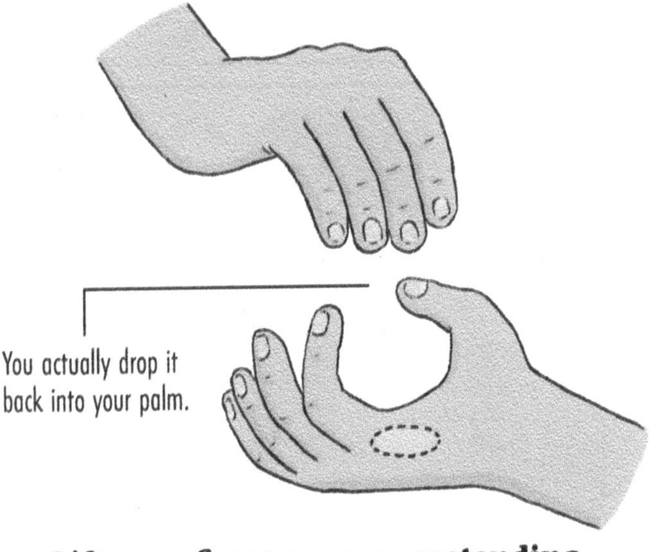

You actually drop it back into your palm.

Lift your fingers away, pretending they are holding the coin.

Now the important bit.

Watch the hand you are pretending has the coin, and look at only this hand for the rest of the trick.

I am blowing the coin away!

You blow on your empty hand.

Now open your empty hand. The coin has 'vanished' into thin air.

This move to make a coin vanish is called the French Drop. If you practise enough, you can do this move sitting right next to someone, and they can't see what has happened.

No one should be looking at the other hand. You can drop it out of sight and hide the coin away.

For the French Drop trick, you need to practise until the movements are so perfect you can do them without thinking. But you also need confidence and misdirection. That's the magicians' term for making sure you focus your audience's attention where you want it. You make them look at the hand you're pretending has the coin, rather than the one it's really in.

The best way to do this is subtly: you focus entirely on your empty hand, and wave it around, while paying no attention at all to the hand that actually has the coin. That makes it easier to hide the coin away.

Now let's think about Houdini's Metamorphosis. He was tied in a sack, and locked into a trunk ... but swapped places with his assistant. How did they misdirect our attention?

They made a fuss about the tied sack, and the locks on the trunk. So what didn't they want us to think about?

For starters, there's the bottom of the sack. There might be a zip to open it.

The other thing is the back of the trunk, or its lid. There must be something that can open in spite of the rope and locks, to let the performer out.

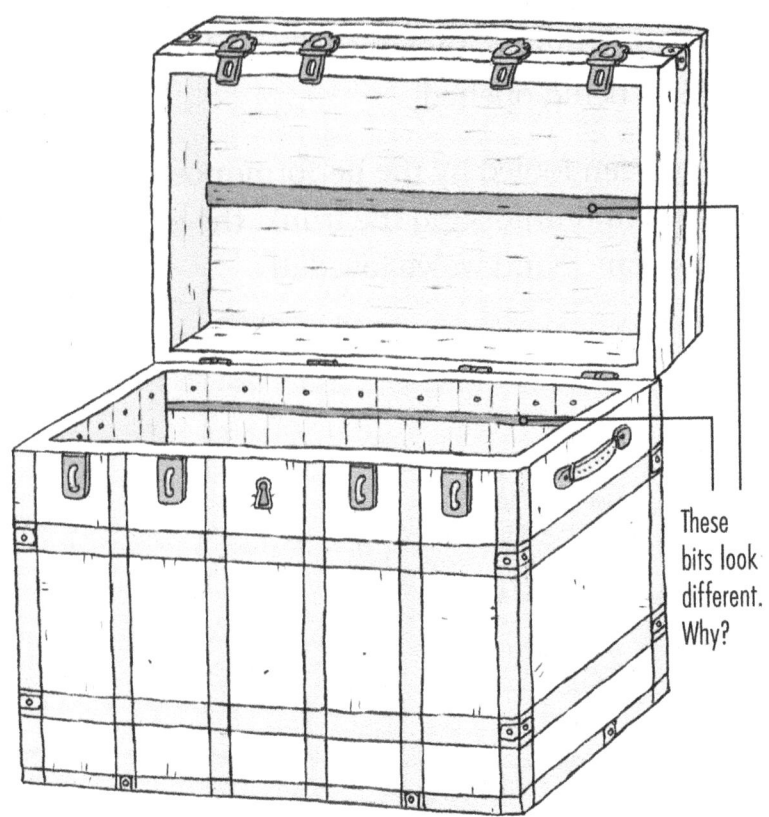

These bits look different. Why?

The moment the trunk's lid is shut, the performer starts getting out of the sack. Once the trunk is locked and roped, they are ready to open it and come out. They are able to swap places with their assistant almost as soon as the curtain is hiding them.

The assistant slips into the trunk while the crowd is clapping, then into the sack while the trunk is being opened.

We've been fooled by the performance of locking and unlocking the trunk, the curtain and so on … and we've loved it!

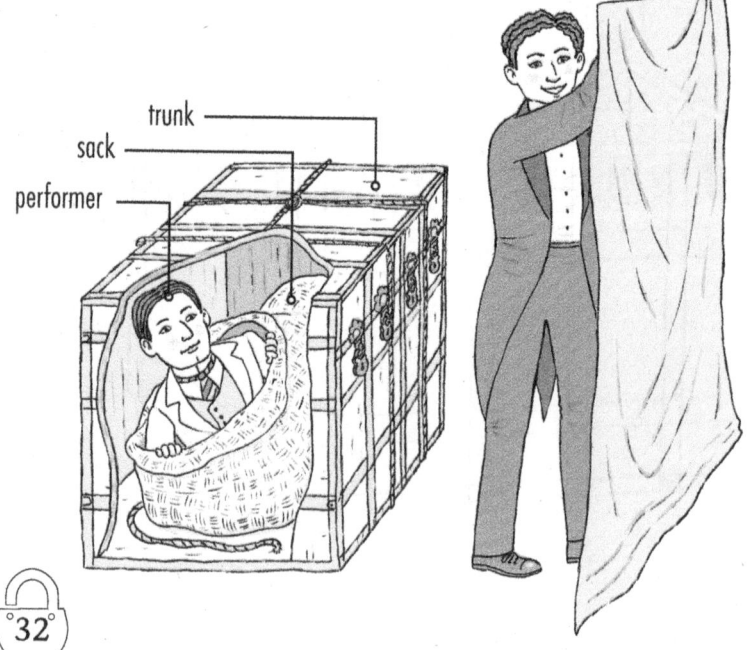

Inventions and ideas

As well as practice, skill, physical fitness and misdirection, Houdini's tricks also needed clever **engineering**. A trick like Metamorphosis simply wouldn't be possible without it.

Why don't we know much about the cunning designs of boxes like the Metamorphosis trunk? Because all magicians agree that they will not give away each other's secrets. So we get only hints of how these **illusions** work.

Tricks like the French Drop are so old, it's all right to show how it's done. If you do it well, everyone will be fooled anyway!

Houdini was an inventor as well as a performer, of course. You can see this from tricks like The Upside Down. He invented this illusion, and he kept its secrets well. All we non-magicians know is that there was a trick to the lid, so the person inside could open it once it was locked down. We still don't know exactly how it worked.

Magicians still keep each other's secrets today. When someone invents a new illusion, no one wants to spoil it! Sometimes they tell us how something works, only to perform it once more with a new twist, and baffle us all over again.

Here's a new version of the Metamorphosis trick.

Houdini used performance skills and misdirection to hide his clever engineering.

He wanted to make The Upside Down very dramatic for the audience, so an assistant with an axe joined him on stage. This assistant was ready to break open the box if necessary, but this was just for show. Houdini knew he could escape more easily than the audience thought.

It would be a very dangerous trick for someone without Houdini's strength and training, though. He still needed to work the mechanism to get out while trapped under water.

Is that all?

Houdini was a star performer, who invented his own illusions. That would be plenty for one person. But there's more!

Houdini was also fascinated by aeroplanes. The world's first-ever aeroplane flight took place in 1903, when he was 29. Seven years later, he had enough money to buy a **biplane** and to take flying lessons.

When he went on tour to Australia later that year, the biplane went on the ship with him and all his equipment. He wanted to be the first person to fly a plane in Australia, and did so in March 1910. Then he sent his plane to England, and never used it again!

As if flying wasn't enough, Houdini started acting in films.

In 1919, he starred in a movie series. This was like a television series, but shown in cinemas in weekly episodes, as television hadn't been invented yet. *The Master Mystery* starred Houdini as a spy who had to battle a robot, survive poison gas and escape daringly from traps.

The Master Mystery wasn't hugely successful, but the film studio went on to create a full-length film starring Houdini. This movie was called *The Grim Game*, and it featured an aeroplane stunt.

Houdini had broken his wrist, so he couldn't do his own stunts in *The Grim Game*. This is how he managed to make it look as if he had:

He stayed on the ground, and someone who was dressed to look like him did the stunts in the air!

Then the film showed Houdini close up just before the **stunt double** dangled from a rope, ready to move between the planes.

The camera showed close-ups of Houdini while the plane was really on the ground ...

dressed the same as Houdini

... and longer shots of the stunt double in the plane and then on the rope.

But then there was an accident. The planes became caught together. Fortunately, the pilots managed to separate the planes and land them, without anyone being hurt.

The whole thing was filmed. The crash was used in the final film, and in publicity.

Houdini said he would pay $1000 to anyone who could prove the plane crash wasn't real. Of course, it was real, so why make the offer? Pure misdirection! It helped to focus people's minds on the actual plane crash, and stop them wondering whether it was really Houdini in the plane.

Being a movie star was definitely good for publicity. Even more people came to see Houdini's shows, so he could charge more for appearing. He took over making his movies, and wrote them as well as starring in them.

These movies were full of escapes and stunts, but they were not as successful as Houdini hoped. He soon realised that making movies was losing him money. He stopped making films in 1923, and carried on performing live instead.

Until then, Houdini had performed as one of many acts in an evening's entertainment. But by 1925, he was such a big star he had his own show.

How did Houdini die?

Houdini made a living doing dangerous things. What's more, his shows always made the most of the danger he put himself in. But he died mainly because when he was ill, he wouldn't go to hospital.

He'd had stomach pains for a while, and a doctor said he had **appendicitis**. Houdini was on tour, and he refused to stop performing. After his show he collapsed and was finally taken to hospital. He died on 31st October 1926.

After Houdini

Although Houdini died many years ago, his name is still famous. He's still admired as a brilliant showman and escapologist. Many modern performers have followed in his footsteps in different ways. Here are a few examples.

Houdini's face

Dorothy Dietrich is an escapologist from Pennsylvania, USA. She has performed some of Houdini's original escapes and helped female escapologists to become more accepted.

American David Copperfield isn't an escapologist, but he built on one of Houdini's bigger tricks. Houdini made an elephant vanish, and in 1983 David Copperfield made the Statue of Liberty disappear.

Mahdi Moudini is an escapologist born in Iran, who now lives and performs in Malaysia.

Lots of other magicians have stage names that end in -ini, in tribute to Houdini. For example, escapologist and strongwoman Cynthia Morrison is known as Cindini, and Italian magician Quintino Marucci performed as Tony Slydini.

Not all escapologists are as skilful as Houdini, and many get injured. They all do what they can to keep the risks low, but escapology is still dangerous.

Houdini had a massive collection of books about magic and publicity posters from famous performers of his time and before. These now belong to collectors and museums.

There is a Houdini museum in Pennsylvania, USA. Dorothy Dietrich performs there and helped the museum find a copy of Houdini's film *The Grim Game*.

A museum called The House of Houdini in Budapest, Hungary, has a number of handcuffs and straitjackets that belonged to Houdini, as well as letters he wrote.

The Houdini Revealed museum in New York, USA, has his Metamorphosis trunk and the robot from *The Master Mystery*.

Houdini is still the most famous escapologist ever. He performed all over the world, in theatres and in movies.

Films have been made about him too. The first movie, made in 1953, pretended that Houdini died doing The Upside Down escape act, even though that's not what really happened. It's a lot more spectacular than dying of appendicitis, and many people still believe that this is how he died.

Houdini gained fame by doing stunts that looked dangerous and ones that really were. He was very good at publicity too. It's hardly surprising that people still talk about him today.

Glossary

appendicitis — an infection in part of your guts that can be cured by an operation

autobiography — a book in which someone famous or important tells their life story

biplane — an early kind of aeroplane with double wings

cell — a small room that a prisoner is locked in to stop them escaping

engineering — designing things to move in particular ways

illusion — something that isn't what it seems to be; a magicians' word for a piece of specially-designed equipment that enables a trick to work, such as the Metamorphosis trunk

rabbi — a Jewish religious leader

restraints — things that stop a person from moving freely, such as handcuffs

straitjacket — a tight piece of clothing with straps, which was sometimes used in the past to prevent people from hurting themselves or others

stunt double — a performer who does stunts in place of someone else, dressed to look like them

stunts — exciting and dangerous actions, often in a performance

Index

Bess (Houdini's wife) 13, 15, 23
Budapest 6, 44
cinema 37
circus 7, 13
crane 19
danger 4, 5, 16, 18, 19, 20, 22, 35, 41, 43, 45
Ehrich Weiss 6–9, 10–11
Eric Weisz 6
films 37, 38, 39, 40, 44, 45
fitness 9, 14, 22, 33
flying 36, 37
French Drop 26–29, 30, 33
handcuffs 14–17, 44
Hungary 4, 6, 44
illusion 33, 34, 36
Metamorphosis 12–13, 14, 30, 33–34, 44
misdirection 30–31, 33, 35, 39
New York 7, 9, 44
padlocks 15
police cells 16
publicity 16, 17, 39, 40, 44, 45
Robert-Houdin, Jean 10
running 9
straitjackets 14, 18, 19, 25, 44
strength 14, 18, 24, 35
stunts 3, 4, 16, 17, 18, 37, 38, 40, 45
Theo (Houdini's brother) 12–13, 25
Upside Down 20, 21, 34, 35, 45

Now answer the questions …

1 What is escapology?

2 Why did another boy say there was no point taking part in a race against Ehrich?

3 'Possibly his most famous trick was when he appeared to send his son to sleep and then made him "float in the air" in front of the audience.' What does the word 'appeared' help you to understand in this sentence?

4 Why did Harry invite journalists to watch him break out of police stations?

5 Why does the author include diagrams of the French Drop trick on pages 26 to 29?

6 How does misdirection help magicians and escapologists to perform tricks?

7 What features does the author use to help readers to stay safe?

8 What kind of performances do you enjoy watching?